394.5
FEN
Fenten

Team behind the great parades

The Team Behind the Great Parades

The Team
Behind
the Great Parades

BY
BARBARA AND D. X. FENTEN

THE WESTMINSTER PRESS
Philadelphia

Book Design by Dorothy Alden Smith

First edition

Published by The Westminster Press®
Philadelphia, Pennsylvania

PRINTED IN THE UNITED STATES OF AMERICA
9 8 7 6 5 4 3 2 1

Library of Congress Cataloging in Publication Data

Fenten, Barbara.
  The team behind the great parades.

  Includes index.
  SUMMARY: Discusses the planning and designing that go into parades around the country, such as the Rose Bowl and Macy's Thanksgiving Day Parade, and describes the work of the many participants, including costumers, musicians, float builders, publicity people, judges, and television teams.
  1. Processions—United States—Juvenile literature.
[1. Parades] I. Fenten, D. X. II. Title.
GT4003.F46   394'.5'0973   81–2981
ISBN 0–664–32682–X   AACR2

Contents

1
Here Comes the Parade

HERE THEY COME. The parade is moving closer. You hear the beat. The drums are pounding in the distance. That's it, the drumbeat. It's getting closer, and as it does, the excitement grows. The beat gets louder, and now you can hear the music. You can't stand still. Your heart begins to beat a little faster. Here comes the parade.

The mounted police are the first to come into view, then the flags swirling in the breeze. Next there's a huge, colorful float. And here's what makes a parade a parade, a high-stepping, free-swinging, drumbeating, fur-hatted band.

From that moment you are caught by the beat of the drums, the rhythm of the music, the antics of the clowns, the beauty of the floats, the fun of the bicycle-riding or roller-skating acts. You're captured by the thrill of the movie, television, and recording stars who pass by waving and smiling, the rock singers doing their latest hits, the horses prancing along as if they knew they were in a parade. Finally, you see the funny little street-sweeping machines that tell you it's all over for another year.

Suddenly you realize you've been staring at this wonderful sight for almost two hours, entranced. There's been no break, no letup, no stopping, no loss of excitement. The parade has been lively, colorful, and entertaining for all that time. With a big smile and a little sigh, you turn for home, the beat of the music that rang in your ears making your steps a little more lively.

It's always a great time for a parade. In California and Texas there are great parades on New Year's Day. In Indiana a parade "steps off" on Memorial Day. Thanksgiving Day brings us great parades in New York, Michigan, and Pennsylvania. It happens all over the country. New Orleans celebrates in March. June is the big month for Anaheim and Orlando. Minneapolis marches in August, and of course July brings out flags and marchers all over the United States. It seems at least once each month there's a great parade to be seen somewhere in our country.

In many places a big parade has become an important part of a holiday tradition. In other places a parade marks a special event or happening. In still other towns and cities parades are held so that everyone can see some special persons or celebrate some very special achievement.

And wherever there is a parade, there are always lots of people. In small towns hundreds of people line the streets to watch their relatives, friends, and neighbors in a small local parade. In large cities hundreds of thousands of people jam together, pressing against police lines, sitting on curbs, perching on shoulders or even climbing trees, sometimes waiting for hours for the big parade to start.

Don't forget the millions more who sit at home in front of television sets, warm and comfortable, happily waiting for a spectacular parade to begin. Everyone is ready, prepared to watch and enjoy every float, every balloon, every clown, every musician, every marcher.

The parade that entertained you for two hours took more

Another great parade comes down
the street
Courier-Journal & Louisville Times Co.

Parade director and staff get started
as much as two years in advance
Macy Special Productions

Director showing sketches of possible
floats to his staff

Miami Tourism Department

than one year to be dreamed up and put together. Nothing was left to chance. The parade director and staff worked full time all year and, toward the end, often worked around the clock. They wanted their parade to thrill and delight you and the millions of other people who watched it. They all worked very hard to make it look very easy, but the job they did was far from easy.

Each of us gets many chances to see great parades, but few get the chance to go behind the scenes to see and meet the teams that plan and design, select and build, and do everything else that's necessary to "put the parade on the street."

Here's your chance to see what it takes, so here we go. Welcome to the team behind the great parades . . .

2

Planning Makes Perfect

FOR EVERY WORTHWHILE ACTIVITY, there must be one special leader, one chief. One person to have the final word, to
run the show. This is the person who gets the praise or the
blame—the pat on the back when everything runs smoothly
or the thumbs-down sign when everything doesn't. If this
carefully chosen leader works very hard, puts in very long
hours, checks on everything, selects and hires the best staff
possible to assist in planning and doing, and is very, very
lucky, everything should go well. When things go well there's
a wonderful parade, a lot of smiling faces, and a great many
pats on the back.

Different parades have different titles for their leader.
Some parade organizations call this person the Director,
while others use the name President. But the title really does-
n't matter too much. Whoever has the title also has plenty of
knowledge, the proper background to run a parade, and
years of experience in parade and spectacle production.

Surprisingly, in a great many cases the Parade Coordinator
—Leader, Director, or President—is not paid for this very
difficult, very time-consuming, very nerve-racking job. In the
case of one truly sensational parade, the president receives no
money—nothing for being president and nothing for all the
years of hard work that led to this top job. But ask and you'll
find out—it isn't done for money, it's done for love, because

The president of the incredible
Tournament of Roses Parade receives
no pay for his enormous responsibility
Tournament of Roses Association

"the parade's the thing."

A good example is the president of that incredible event
called the Tournament of Roses Parade, which steps off early
in the morning every New Year's Day in Pasadena, California. The parade is produced by the Tournament of Roses
Association, which has more than 1,400 members who give
more than 60,000 hours of volunteer work each year to put
on this spectacular event. All are volunteers, none are paid,
and they all believe that "their" parade is the greatest in the
world. Some of the hardest workers move up through the
ranks, doing all sorts of jobs, until they become the top officers
who actually plan and take full responsibility for the entire
parade.

Getting to be president takes years and years of service and
work. One recent president was named to the post after
being in the organization for twenty-one years. He had been

Dallas Cowboys coach, Tom Landry,
rides up the parade route as Grand
Marshal of the Mardi Gras Parade
Cotton Bowl Council

a member of fifteen committees and chairperson of six. Another member, who had served as president several years before, had also been a volunteer for twenty-one years. He had gotten "the parade bug" watching as a boy, climbing the pepper trees along the parade route so he could see. As a young boy he worked with youth organizations decorating floats, and later, as a college student, he marched in the parade.

A new president's job starts almost as soon as the street sweepers have cleared the streets from the last parade. Choosing a theme and choosing a Grand Marshal are the top items on the list of "things to do." Both decisions are difficult but delightful for the incoming president. Everyone is invited to send in suggestions for the theme of the parade. Last year the winner was picked from more than 7,000 entries sent in

14

from every one of the fifty states. The person who suggests the winning theme is invited to attend the parade, the Rose Bowl game, and many other exciting events during Rose Bowl week.

Very soon after these two important decisions are made, the president packs a bag and starts off on a series of goodwill trips that will cover more than 50,000 miles. Along with the usual luggage, the president carries information on the newly chosen theme for the upcoming parade, a copy of the latest parade film, and color portraits to give to the organizations that were in previous parades. High on the list of "musts" is a visit to each city from which a band has been invited to march in the next parade. The president will congratulate the members and tell them things they didn't know about the event. The president will not return to Pasadena for almost three months—sometime in July, very tired, but also very happy and very enthusiastic.

The Harborfields High School
Marching Band and Drill Team
auditions before the parade director

D. X. Fenten

The president of the Tournament of Roses Parade heads a large team, including 29 committees, each led by a different chairperson, and each responsible for a different and very special job. This executive committee team handles all aspects of the parade, starting at the very beginning and continuing to the very end. Some of the responsibilities, such as judging, queen and court, television and radio, and float entries, are obvious. But imagine a separate committee just for horseback riders (Equestrians), for the sites where the floats are decorated (Decorating Places), and even for any food that must be served to workers and paraders (Food Services). It is easy to see that a full team must work very, very hard to put on a truly great Tournament of Roses Parade.

Other parades have other teams and other ways of getting a great parade "on the street." Because the people who run these parades are paid, the sponsors cannot afford to have nearly so large an organization, nor do they get so many people with years of dedicated service. For example, many of the "big city" parades sponsored by department stores or other large organizations put on their big shows with only a very hardworking director, an assistant director or two, and a small staff of paid workers. To be certain their companies are "getting their money's worth," this small group of people may also be responsible for other events staged by their company during the year.

These professional parade makers divide up the work, carefully spread out the responsibility, and, despite the ever-increasing panics and pressures, manage to produce a spectacular and exciting show each year.

During the judging for prizes, the artist's original sketch is compared with the final float

Tournament of Roses Association

Heading the Right Way!

serrurier & associates   Dr Pepper

When a small staff does the parade, there is a lot of overlapping. A few people often work together on each problem or task. They help each other in times of need, checking ideas with workers in other areas and generally cooperating so all the jobs get done. In the case of another truly great parade, the Macy's Thanksgiving Day Parade in New York City, the leader responsible for just about everything is called the Special Productions Director. The assistant, called the Associate Director, also acts as the Parade Manager. One member of the top-level staff for this parade is called the Band Coordina-

This band, chosen by the band
coordinator, has waited and worked
almost two years for this moment
Donna Ruth Feinstein

These three lucky bands appear
twice, once in the evening parade
and the next day in the half-time
show at the Orange Bowl
Miami Tourism Department

tor, but that job covers a great deal more than just the music.

Though the Special Productions Director has the last word
on everything, the job consists of constant meetings with the
others and sharing ideas and decisions. A typical meeting of
the Special Productions Department starts early in the day,
runs late, and covers item after item. Some of the items are
big and some small, some important and some trivial, but all
are a part of what makes a parade great.

One of these meetings takes place in early April. There are
a great many things to discuss and decide, for there are only
eight more months until the parade "steps out." First, there
is a discussion of the circus that top staff members saw the

The Olympics float thrills millions of
people, thanks to Texas Instruments
Cotton Bowl Council

previous day. They went, not to watch and enjoy the show, but to discover new ideas they can use in their own parade. "Remember," the director said, "we're looking for ideas that will add a little something extra, something special to our parade. We never want to take the chance of people becoming bored by seeing the same things year after year. We're looking for small changes, not big ones. You know, the kind that may just add a laugh or two."

They all offer and discuss many ideas, then go on to other matters. Each time a decision has to be made—on costumes, floats, celebrities to be invited, bands—the staff members have their say. They hold a discussion, then the director makes the decision.

Usually, directors of large parades have creative arts backgrounds, training, and education. This may include work in advertising, public relations, promotion, or, in the media, on newspapers, magazines, or radio and television. Such training comes in very handy. Each marvelous, great parade is really a giant advertisement for a store, a place, or an event. Each parade is brilliantly produced, excitingly entertaining, and perfectly engineered.

All of this is the direct result of the efforts of a team of very hardworking people. This team makes sure everything is perfect. People must be dressed, floats must be decorated beautifully, and both people and floats must have the right background music when they appear before millions of watchers. Imagine the care it takes to run such a parade, one that will be seen by 1½ million people on the street and more than 125 million on television. If getting a parade ready sounds like a gigantic task, it is. It requires the time and the talents of many people. The director and top staff are the cement that holds the entire operation together. The people to whom they turn for all the other skills they need are the team behind any great parade.

3
Designing the Fabulous Floats

WILL THE FLOAT BE BEAUTIFUL . . . in the street, on television? Will it do what it is supposed to do? Will it be within the rules of the parade? Will it start? Will it run? Will it go the whole way?

Just as soon as the parade director and staff get started on a new parade, so do the designers, the engineers, and the technicians. These people, men and women from all over the country, form the team that gets the floats started on their way into a parade.

In some organizations the designers must wait until the parade theme is announced. In others they get started just as soon as the floats come back to the warehouse after a parade. The floats must be checked, rated, and graded to see how well they did, and whether they can be improved the next time they go out.

Parade designers are a very special group of people. They must have soaring imaginations that allow them to create floats to be enjoyed by all kinds of people of all ages. They must be craftspersons, because the floats they design must be able to move down an entire parade route, no matter what the weather, and still work as well and look as good as when they started. Parade designers must be sticklers for details so their floats are 100 percent within the rules set down by the parade sponsors. All the while they dream and sketch and

The extraordinary imagination of the
float designer created this dramatic
float

Miami Tourism Department

design, they wonder: Will it start? Will it run? Will it go the
whole way?

Each parade has rules and regulations that challenge the
talent and the skill of the designers. For example, the floats
for the Macy's Thanksgiving Day Parade are made in a studio
in New Jersey, across the river from New York City. To get
from New Jersey to New York, the floats must go through one
of the tunnels under the Hudson. This means that the floats

can be no higher than 12 feet 6 inches and no wider than 8 feet. That's very small for a parade float. For the parade itself, the floats can be as wide as 24 feet, as high as 40 feet, and as long as 32 feet.

With this information in mind, the designers and engineers have dreamed up beautiful floats that fold down to the required size. This is an extra added problem for the designers, but they have come up with solutions. Their amazing solutions result not only in beautiful floats but in floats that fold to fit into the tunnels, open up to very large sizes for the parade, and then fold down again for the trip back to their home base in New Jersey.

The clever designers who work their magic on "folding floats," do a similar job of transforming floats that have already been in the parade into new floats, floats no one would recognize as old ones. Since floats are so expensive to build, it is important that the greatest possible use be made of each one. If you see a huge bunny rabbit in a parade one year, you might see the same float, or at least the insides of it, the next year, but now the bunny is a huge polar bear, a big monkey, or one of Darth Vader's soldiers.

Sometimes the designers, engineers, and builders of floats convince the sponsors that they need bigger and better routes for their bigger and better floats. Several years after the first Indianapolis 500 Parade the floats became so big they couldn't get around the curves at the circle in the center of

This float, from a previous parade, is
being rebuilt for this year's parade
Devore Floats, Dale Swope

This jeep will be completely hidden
when the float is finished
Tournament of Roses Association

25

town. Not only were the floats quite large, but they had attachments, called outriggers, that made them even larger. It took the parade a lot longer than usual one year because the float drivers had to jockey the huge creations very slowly and very carefully around the curves. The following year the parade committee had a choice. They could either put size limits on the designers or they could find a route that was wide enough for the largest floats. They chose to move the parade to a new route.

The teams that come up with the ideas and then the plans for the Tournament of Roses Parade present a completely different set of problems to the designers, engineers, and drafters. Each float is self-propelled, so the engineers must include in their plans a stripped-down jeep or truck, usually hidden underneath. But that's only the beginning. Because the parade moves along at a very slow 2½ miles per hour, the engines get very hot. So the engines must be redesigned to include extra-large radiators for cooling. Because of these extra-large radiators, designers must provide space for a spare water tank. It is hot and exhausting work to drive these huge floats, and drivers are unable to see very much. The designers must allow room for an extra driver and for a telephone link between the drivers and an outside observer. In addition, the designers put on a special tow bar, just in case the top-condition engine should decide to quit.

But that's for the part of the float that no one sees. There are very specific rules for the top of the float too. Unlike the New York parade, the Pasadena parade does not need floats that fold, because there are no tunnels to pass through. The floats for this parade can be much larger, but none can be more than 16 feet high, 18 feet wide, and 50 feet long. The fact that the float doesn't have to fold makes the designing and engineering a little easier, but the rest of the strict rules do not.

Here's how reporters covering the parade were told about the rules. "Basically, the floats should be covered with

Every inch must be covered with
flowers or something that grew
Tournament of Roses Association

flowers, because this is really a floral parade. But we don't
limit the designers only to flowers. Every inch of every float
must be covered with something that grew, and these materials must be put on the float exactly as they grew. Nothing
must be done to the materials to change them. For example,
it's perfectly all right to use coffee beans on a float. As you
know, they are green. But if they are roasted and brown, they
cannot be used. Raw rice and all sorts of seeds can be used,
just as they came from nature."

To follow these instructions, designers learn the colors of
many, many flowers, how long they last, and how many are
required to cover a square inch. The designers also learn as
much as they can about a wide variety of other natural
materials. When they start their designs, they work with all
these materials in mind.

But that's only the "basic" float. The thing that makes a

The animation of the Cal Poly float
makes millions smile
California Polytechnic Institute

parade like the Rose Parade truly great is the extra-special
floats. One of the best displays of teamwork comes from a
group of college students at Cal Poly (California Polytechnic
Institute), whose float year after year wins the prize for best
animation. Their floats are full of action, always presenting
the kinds of things that put a smile on every face that sees
them.

The animation team is made up of designers, engineers,
computer scientists, hydraulics experts, and construction
people, to name just a few. They work together for months
designing the float, the mechanics, and the engineering necessary to make their display do what they want it to do. They
must design in, and leave space for, hundreds and hundreds
of feet of pipe, hose, and cable underneath their float. For this
team, hydraulics makes everything go. For each movement,
big or small, there must be two hydraulic lines on the float—
one line to bring the fluid under pressure up from the pump,
the other to take it back after its job has been done.

The valves needed to control the flow of the fluid and the animation of the float can't be controlled by hand. So the team designs a small but sophisticated computer to do the job. This computer acts as the brains of the entire animation system on the huge Cal Poly float. It senses each and every move at exactly the right moment. Then it delivers its electronic message to the proper location on the float, so that everything moves exactly as the team designed it to move.

The computer signals bear cubs to stand, to turn, to dance. It signals a bee to land. It signals every one of hundreds of movements each time the float goes through a complete animation cycle.

Is it any wonder that the design team breathes a sigh of relief when the float is tested several days before parade day? The team breathes a bit easier when the float is tested early in the morning on the day of the parade. Then the team starts to wonder. Will it start? Will it run? Will it go the whole way?

4

Creating the Colorful Costumes

SHEETS OF THIN PAPER cover the floor. A man and a woman sit in the middle of the papers, each sketching rapidly on a pad. They look up at a drawing of a float standing close by, sketch a while, look at the drawing, sketch some more, then tear off the sheet and sketch some more. They have been doing this for quite some time and have collected a large pile of the thin sheets of paper.

This is the final stage of a process that has taken these costume designers months to reach. It will still be several weeks before the first piece of cloth can be cut and the first sequins or feathers can be sewn on the costumes for the parade. Since there are more than a thousand people in a large parade, there are many costumes that must be designed and made, others remodeled from a previous year, and even some that are rented from a costume rental company.

Parade costumers usually get their experience making costumes for other kinds of shows, the theater, television, or even for the circus. While each type of show has its own special problems, certain things about every kind of costume-making are pretty much the same. Float costumes must match exactly the theme of the parade or float, give viewers an idea of the season represented by the float, and show the time and place where the scene is supposed to be. When the float depicts the South in the 1860's, the costumes must be

Designs for these costumes were
researched carefully to fit in with the
theme of this float

Tournament of Roses Association

long and full and made of materials used at that time. When
the theme is western, then cowboy gear is in order.

The real key to good costumes is that they must not call
attention to themselves. The costumes and the individuals
who wear them are part of a whole impression, a whole feel-
ing, and it is important that people watching the parade look
at the scene as a whole and not just at the costumes.

When the costumers think their designs have captured the
true spirit of the parade and of the specific float, they send
their sketches, usually with pieces of the fabric to be used
attached, to the parade director. After a few conferences,
some phone calls back and forth, perhaps a few additional
sketches, some even in color, the costume makers are ready
to begin.

Along with all the usual requirements for costumers, certain parades and certain situations add special problems. For
example, in both Disneyland and Disney World, there is a

This costume was tried on many
times before the parade so the horse
could get used to it

New Orleans Times-Picayune

parade every night for months. This is quite different from a Rose Parade or a Thanksgiving Day Parade that marches only once a year. For the parade that takes place many times, the costume designer must be certain that the costumes are not only pretty, colorful, and exciting, but in addition they must be strong enough to stand the wear and tear of everyday use. They must be able to take the strain of being put on, worn, taken off, hung up, and having all that done over again about 120 times.

The viewers and the wearers are not the only ones to be considered when costumes are made. If there are animals in the parade, their likes and dislikes must be considered or there could be trouble. That's why a performer will always wear a new costume several times before the show so the animals can see it and get used to it. Then they won't be scared and startled into bolting, bucking, or acting skittish during the performance.

And, of course, there are also the performers' superstitions. Some people think certain colors are bad luck, others think certain materials bring bad luck. Rarely will you see peacock feathers or the color green used where performers who have worked in the circus are to appear. They feel these things are bad luck, so costume designers stay far away from them.

But costume designers are not only responsible for creating the costumes you see on the floats. In a parade like the Macy's Thanksgiving Day Parade, where there are at least 2,500 marchers, the costume designers also make some of the props for the clowns, coverall outfits for the balloon holders, and everything else that is worn or used in the parade, whether it is used by a person, an animal, or even a machine. Sometimes these special jobs really tax the talents of the designers, but more often than not, if you ask them, they will just shrug and say, "It's the oddball things, the different things, that really make this kind of designing fun."

It would seem that once the designers had designed the costumes and the costume makers had made them, their jobs

The designers of these costumes had
great imagination and a lot of empty
bleach bottles and paper plates
New Orleans Times-Picayune

would be completed. However, in many cases, this is only the beginning. The costumes must be fitted on the people, and they must fit right if they are to be worn comfortably. If the parade is held during the cold part of the year, there must be a little extra room so the person or the performer can wear heavy underwear. If the parade is held in a warm area, the material must be light and cool and must not show the stains of perspiration. Wherever the parade is held, the costume must be comfortable so the performer can move in it, wave, and do anything that must be done during the march.

Once the event is over and the costumes are not needed again for a while, the designers must check them out to see how they made it through the parade. Really good designers remember the best fabrics, the best ornaments, the best designs, so they can be used again when it's designing time for a new parade.

5

Music, Music, Music

"BOY, I DON'T ENVY YOU. Picking the bands for the parade is one job that's really tough," she said. They were landing in Iowa as part of their swing through the states to see and hear bands for the upcoming parade. She was the "hear" part of the team; he was the "see" part. She carried a list of all the bands that had written to the parade director asking to be considered for a spot in the parade. Next to most of the names there were notes, checks, dots, and other coded signs. Before this team of two would be through with their trip they would have visited all the bands that still had a chance to be in the big parade. This trip, by plane, train, bus, and car, was the last of a series of trips over a period of two years.

"Sometimes," he said with a smile, "I don't envy myself either. For most of the other decisions on the parade we get all sorts of help. We get together, kick the subject around, then when we have pretty well discussed everything and given our preferences, our director makes the final decision. But with this, it's different. We're looking for bands that not only sound great but look great too. We require a lot more than just good sound. After we see and hear all these bands, we make the decision. Sure, we tell the other assistant directors what we think, and they might offer an opinion, but the decision is left up to us. It's not easy, not easy at all. Especially when you see so many really great bands."

Bake sales, car washes, baby-sitting,
lawn mowing, and raffles helped earn
the thousands of dollars needed to get
this band across the country to this
parade

Courier-Journal & Louisville Times Co.

Letters pour into the music director's office all year long.
Small bands, big bands, formal bands, comedy bands, drum
and bugle corps, fife and drum bands, all-brass bands, steel
drum bands, and many many more. There are Teen Tour
bands, Patriot bands, Marching Show bands, Pirate bands,
Kiltie Marching bands, Navy, Army, and Marine bands, and

many other bands. More than 4,000 musicians are needed for the large parades, and they must be picked from among the hundreds of bands that send letters, photos, and tapes.

A few of the bands need no picking. For example, the Salvation Army Band, which makes most of its instruments, has appeared in the Rose Parade more than sixty times. And the McDonald's All-American High School Band has played in both the Rose Parade and the Macy's Thanksgiving Day Parade every year since the band was organized. This band of 100 members—two of the best high school musicians from each of the fifty states—is formed into an outstanding marching band.

While there is a great deal of teamwork in every part of putting on a parade, it probably shows the most in the area of music. Often this teamwork may cover as much as two years. For large bands to appear across the country far from their homes, a lot of money is needed. In the latest parade, it cost about $90,000 to transport a band from the East to the West Coast. Since all this money must be raised by the band, 18 months to 2 years are allowed before an appearance.

It all starts with a request to the parade director to appear in a parade. When the letters, music tapes, and photos are in, the parade leaders check everything, eliminate some groups, and keep the others in a "ready to go" file. From the hundreds of requests to appear, the Rose Parade picks 24 bands, while the Macy's Thanksgiving Day Parade picks an even smaller number—14. Later discussions and eliminations in the parade offices whittle the number down even further.

Before the final choices are made, each of the "possible" bands is visited. The band puts on its entire show, just the way it would look and sound in the parade. The band is checked very carefully. Everything must be perfect, or as close to perfect as anyone can get. Uniforms must match and be of a kind that will look good on television. Marching and "dancing" routines must be crisp, attractive, and exciting to watch. And the music must be the best in the country. This is no time

The television producer suggested
painting the road so the bands would
"stand out"

Cotton Bowl Council

for excuses or nervousness. Many of the bands have been
practicing their music and routines daily for weeks and
weeks. They must be perfect for the audition, just as for the
parade.

For the final audition, the music directors are joined on
their visits to the bands by the producer from the television
network that will carry the parade. This group watches carefully as the musicians go through their routines. Unless there
is some glaring problem or error, the band is then told it is
in the parade.

Once the cheering and shouting have died down, the two teams get together. The band goes through its routine once more and the parade people watch. Then they have meetings so that everything about the parade and the band's part in the parade is understood.

Checking over their list, the music directors sit over coffee with the band's director, the band's squad leaders, and the television producer. The music director in charge of appearance makes some suggestions about the band's uniforms. The television producer agrees. He says, "If it is possible and not too expensive, your uniforms would look even nicer with some sort of scarf at the neckline." Heads all around the table shake in agreement, and the band director adds this suggestion to his notes.

"O.K.," says one music director. "I guess that about does it. Let's check one more time just to be sure. You understand all the instructions about the dates, getting to the parade, the numbers you are to do, and the amount of time each is to take? You understand all our guidelines for the parade? You'll incorporate some of the changes we've suggested and keep working on them until you have them down pat? Be extra careful about the timing. As our friend here will tell you, television time must be perfect. We can't allow anyone to exceed the allotted time. Everything must go on, but even more important, everything must go off on time."

Once again there is agreement all around the table. Now it is the other music director's turn to speak. "Once you join us at the parade, there'll be plenty of work, but we'll see to it that it's not all work and no play. Our office is preparing the band kits now, and just as soon as they are ready, we'll send them to you. We want every member of every band to have a great time in our city. First, the kit will have a list of good hotels and the prices they charge. Then we'll put in some discount cards for restaurants, movies, and special events, as well as a whole list of special sightseeing trips for the band members. If there's anything else you think you might need,

40

just let us know. We'll get the kits out to you in plenty of time for you to plan your trip and the ways you'll raise the money to come to the parade."

Heads shake up and down in agreement when she stops talking. After much handshaking the parade people get up to leave, escorted to the car by the band director. The squad leaders remain at the table. "We've got to organize car washes, flower sales, lawn mowings, a giant barbecue, fresh fruit sales—we need in the neighborhood of $90,000 to get there, that's some neighborhood—candy sales, Christmas cards, concerts . . ."

6

Building the Behemoths

TEAMWORK, TEAMWORK, TEAMWORK. All over the country there are teams working to make this parade "their" parade, the best one ever. In small towns and big cities band members work to get ready and to raise the money for their trip to the parade. In between costume fittings and alterations everyone pitches in to help with bake sales, car washes, and anything else that will raise money. Kick lines practice until they ache, then they practice some more.

The designers complete work on their sketches for the floats, the props, the costumes, and many other things. After discussion and approval, they go on to do the color renderings. Once the color renderings, or drawings, are finished and approved, in special shops in various parts of the country the building of floats and balloons begins. Everywhere groups of people work together and work hard to get the parade "on the street."

Now it is time for other teams to take over. First there will be carpenters and welders, then experts with wire mesh, plaster, and plastic. The new teams are the actual builders, the people who will turn a dream from a piece of paper into something colorful, exciting, magnificent, and worthy of a great parade.

There are, of course, several ways to make floats and balloons, depending, usually, on the materials used. Let's go back to the students at Cal Poly and see how they operate once their design team has done its job.

They start with a stripped-down truck chassis and build a frame pretty close to the final shape of the float. Looking at it, you might be able to tell it is some sort of animal, but you certainly can't be sure. Into this framework is carefully put a mass of hardware, pipes, hoses, and all the other parts needed to make the float move. Carpenters work with hydraulics people, electricians, and engineers to be certain everything will function as it should.

Next on the scene are the welders. They put into place and secure the supporting rods that hold up the "skin." All the rods, rings, and other parts that give the shape to the float are welded into place. It's like a giant model kit, with everything going into place, step by step, and each person doing one job best.

With all the basic shape parts in place, the mesh is attached. This woven metal cloth, very much like one-inch chicken wire, is pushed, pulled, and shaped to follow every line, every detail, every curve that appears on the engineer's drawings and on the designer's sketches. Many trips are made back and forth between these drawings and the float. This is no place for anyone to make a mistake. Everything has to be perfect. A little carelessness—a little poor workmanship here, a bulge there, a missed curve—and the appearance of the float could be ruined. Everyone is extra careful and everyone checks and double-checks everyone else's work. It would never do to give an ape a hump or a snake a lump.

Once the meshing is complete, the float starts to come to life. Now you can tell not only that it is going to be an animal, you can tell the kind of animal. When this is done, it is time for the next members of the team, the next specialists, to come in and do their job. Using large compressed-air spray guns, the cocooners cover all the spaces in the wire mesh with a plastic spray. This liquid plastic comes out of the nozzle looking like giant cobwebs, but when it hits the metal mesh,

43

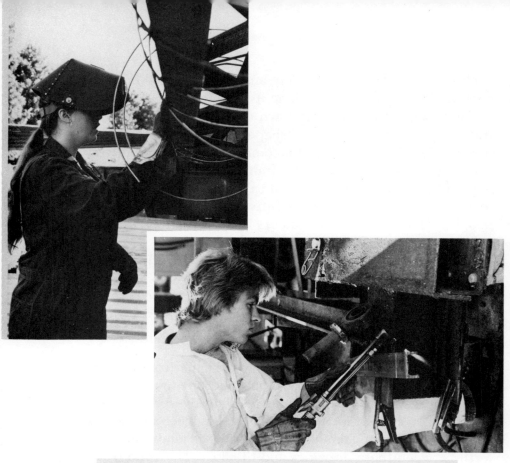

Carpenters and welders begin the
task of building the float
California Polytechnic Institute

44

it becomes a plastic film which hardens instantly into a smooth, brilliant-white skin. That's why it's called cocooning. Now the float really starts to look like something besides a mess of wire, tubes, and pipes. It starts to look more like a parade float and less like an engineer's nightmare.

But the cocoon is white, making the whole float pure white. So here come the painters. The float will be painted in all the correct colors the designers chose. It must be exact, so that the float itself will be the guide for the next team that arrives on the scene, the flower pasters. Once again, in the painting stage, everyone is especially careful. This is another one of the places where something could go wrong. Just to be sure, the painters keep checking the drawing made so many months before by the designers and engineers.

For the Rose Parade, there are now only about 48 hours left to go. Here come the flower pasters. They come in teams, ready to work and to work hard. Up to 350,000 fresh flowers are needed to cover some of the floats. There are two ways of putting on the flowers. The first way is called "picking in," and it's done with delicate flowers such as roses, orchids, and carnations. Each flower must first be placed in a small plastic tube filled with water and a special chemical that keeps the flower in perfect bloom for about three days. Then the tubes are sunk into the cocoon, or skin, of the float. The other flowering system is a bit simpler. Here, the flowers, or usually just the petals, are pasted right onto the float. To do the job, glue that has the preserving chemical mixed right in is used. The petals are put on, one petal at a time.

All the flower pasters are members of youth groups, including boy scouts and girl scouts, church groups, and others. They are all volunteers and work without pay, though their organizations are paid by the float-building companies. Flowering is a sought-after job, and the ninth-graders through twelfth-graders come back year after year after year.

One organization has the words PETAL PUSHERS imprinted on sweat shirts for its team members. A different color

Wire mesh is pulled, bent, and
stapled into place

California Polytechnic Institute

is used each year, and everyone can see who has been flowering longest. There are all degrees of "rattiness." Some of the shirts are stained, some are patched, some are cut off at the elbows, some are worn, and some are brand-new. Every shirt is worn by someone willing to work long and hard on "their" float.

They come early in the morning and stay until late at night. They bring bags of lunches and thermoses of hot chocolate. They bring cake, cookies, Cokes, and their good spirits and dedication to get the job done, beautifully.

Each group is assigned a single float and works on that float until it is completed. Hour after hour after hour the work goes on. The team members work, they eat, they work, they talk, they work, they sing, they work and they work and they do the job.

Describing her experience, Donna, a high school junior who had always "wanted to be a part of that parade," says,

The plastic spray makes the shape
start to come to life
Tournament of Roses Association

"My fingers were so numb, I could hardly tell what I was
doing. The building had become quite cold and damp and
there were still plenty of flowers to paste. My fingers were
frozen in the permanent position of holding the head of a
flower. I was like some sort of automatic machine. I'd reach
down with these frozen fingers, pick up the flower, press it
into the glue, and place it on the float Just like a machine.
Pick, press, push. Pick, press, push. It seemed there was no
end to the number of flowers that had to be glued. Cold,

Finishing touches!
Devore Floats, Dale Swope

miserable—pick, press, push. It was fantastic and I can't wait
to do it again next year."

Floats for other parades use other materials instead of
flowers. Some use papier-mâché over the wire mesh, and still
others use vinyl paper stuffed into the mesh spaces. Tissue
paper was once used for the float decoration, but it took only
a little bit of rain to ruin all the work. Now, with vinyl paper
for the petals, flowers, and other decorations and papier-
mâché for the large parts of the characters, these floats can
go anywhere in any kind of weather.

If you are a balloon maker, you think about weather. While

a little too much wind can cause some anxious moments, your creations fly, rain or shine. In the balloon-making team effort, it all starts when someone dreams up an idea for a huge balloon. The designers take the idea and make it into drawings and plans. From these, model makers make wax models. Using a wax model that looks exactly the way they want the

Balloon designer working from a wax model of Kermit

Goodyear Aerospace Corporation

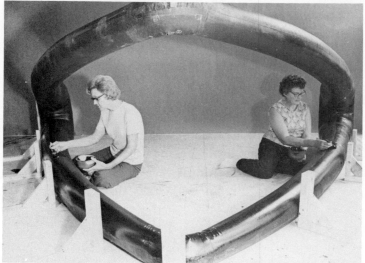

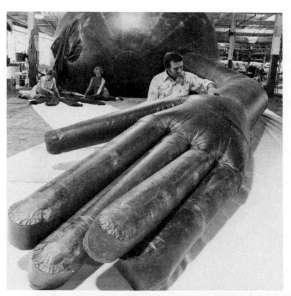

The pattern is traced and cut out,
then a special coating seals the seams.
Kermit's big mouth gets a coat of
white paint, a second one of green
Goodyear Aerospace Corporation

Part of the team that made Kermit
poses with him before his first test
flight

balloon to look, engineers, designers, and drafters make detailed drawings. The drawings are then enlarged and used as pattern pieces for the balloon. For Kermit the Frog there are 72 different pattern pieces for the balloon, which measures 63 feet high and 24 feet wide. It takes the design team about a month to make the blueprints and then the patterns, which are used just like the patterns of a dressmaker.

Other members of the team cut out the rubberized fabric for the balloon. Rubber cement holds the parts together. When all the parts have been glued, there are fourteen separate compartments of this paper-thin fabric to be filled with helium. After being tested to see that the glue has held, the balloon is inflated and painted with special paint. First, white paint goes on to cover the rubber, then the real color of the balloon. Painters use brushes and rollers. At last the balloon goes out for test-flying. After everyone is sure it is ready, it is packed in a wooden box until the night before the parade.

The teams have completed their jobs. The floats, the props, the costumes, the bands—everything is ready and waiting. All the specialists have worked together to make a whole bunch of dreams come true. Now it's time for some other teams to work together to get those dreams out "on the street."

7

Training Good Leaders

MARSHALS AND CAPTAINS. A big parade needs leaders, good leaders, so that everything goes off as planned. They make it look easy, but it's really not. Many, many hours of conferences and training are required to make a good leader for a parade. Leaders are a part of the parade team that is on the scene but doesn't stand out. In fact, if everything goes according to plan, you might not even know the leaders are there.

Because these people are so important to a parade, they are usually chosen many months before the parade so there will be plenty of time to train them. If their titles matched their jobs, they would be called "On-the-Street Directors." They are part of the parade, marching or riding with their sections. Then, if something should go wrong, marshals and captains are right on the spot to make corrections.

Usually selected from among the people who have been in the parade many times before, the marshals and captains are the key to a successful parade.

Standing in front of a group of these leaders, the parade director explains the jobs they will be doing: "You people can make the difference between a great parade and one that has all sorts of problems. You've heard it before—putting on a parade is a team effort. It takes all kinds of people doing all kinds of things to make it go, and make it go properly."

The people in the room are all volunteers—they will not be

This parade captain is having fun but
is also "right on the spot," to help if
anything goes wrong
Courier-Journal & Louisville Times Co.

paid, and they all love parades. All of these men and women
have marched in previous parades and some have been street
leaders. The director continues: "Your jobs are more important than those of anyone else once that parade starts moving.
You have to keep it moving. You have to keep it on time. You
have to keep it exciting. You have to solve any problems. And
you have to do all these things without the viewers noticing.

"Those of you who haven't done it before, remember that
marshals and captains do all the parade-directing on the
street. Every part of the parade, every unit, every person in
the parade reports to a captain. We usually have a captain for
each band, one for each float, a few for the clowns and other
people marching, and several spotted along the parade route
to help out in the event of any kind of emergency. We figure

55

These volunteers are well padded
with warm clothing under their
costumes

Donna Ruth Feinstein

there are about eight sections to our parade, and each of these
has its own captain. About nine or ten of these captains report
to each marshal.

"There are a great many things that you'll be doing as you
march along with the parade, but one thing comes first. We
have a great many people in our parade, and their safety is
the most important thing of all. You are the people who
guarantee that a good and safe time will be had by everyone.
Suppose a float gets stuck or a band member hurts an ankle.
Remember, the parade keeps marching. Just as soon as something happens, the marcher tells the captain. If it is minor, the
captain takes care of it without any halt to the parade. If it

looks as if the parade may have to be stopped, the captain tells the marshal. It's the marshal's job to get the right help—help that can solve the problem, quickly and quietly."

The captains and marshals listening to the director start to applaud. The director raises one hand and the applause stops. "That's the spirit," the director says, "but hold your applause until the end, until we see the terrific kind of job you all actually carry through. Right now we've got a lot of training to do. We've got to think ahead to all the things that can go

Getting Snoopy ready to make his appearance

Donna Ruth Feinstein

Heavy nets control Kermit until the
wind dies down

Goodyear Aerospace Corporation

wrong and show you how to solve all these problems."

Throughout the hours of training, one point becomes very clear. No matter what happens, the captains and the marshals have to "keep calm and use their heads." It is impossible to try to think of everything that can happen. There is always the unexpected.

During one coffee break, the captains were standing and talking. "Do you remember the time we nearly lost one of the balloons?" one asked. Another captain smiled. "If it hadn't been for some quick thinking by Cheryl, old Kermit would have been a goner."

It was early in the morning on parade day and it was time to raise the balloons. Each person held a handle attached to a long piece of rope. At the other end of the rope was Kermit. The nets were removed from the balloon and it lifted slowly into the air. It looked great up there, swaying gently.

Just as the handlers started to move forward, there was a gust of wind. Each of them realized immediately that this giant balloon didn't want to be held. They all held on tightly, pulled down firmly as the wind died. Kermit was quiet again.

Just as they all started to breathe normally, a new gust of wind hit the balloon. Kermit suddenly moved up and sideways and slammed into a building. Some of the handlers lost their ropes as the balloon jerked upward. They ran over to other handlers and helped with their ropes. Several ran for Cheryl, who was instructing another group nearby.

As soon as she saw what was happening, she acted. She called to all the marchers nearby to help. In seconds clowns and dancers, jugglers and roller skaters were holding and pulling on the ropes. It was a large team of people against Kermit, and Kermit was winning.

Cheryl knew she needed help and needed it quickly. A few more slams against the building and Kermit would be ruined. She ran to the delivery trucks and shouted to the drivers. They each grabbed one of the dangling ropes and tied it to their trucks. Kermit kept swinging wildly. When the ropes were tied, Cheryl shouted the order, and the trucks slowly started to pull the balloon away from the building. It took only a few seconds and few people saw it, but this captain had saved the big balloon so it could fly in the parade just as if nothing had happened.

8

I Always Wanted to Be in a Parade

SO FAR, SOME CHIEFS, but no Indians. The parade team had all the leaders it needed, but it didn't have the "regular" people it needed. Where would the clowns come from? Where do you get balloon handlers? How do you find and convince radio, movie, television, and recording stars to appear on a holiday weekend without pay?

The answer to all these questions is the same—volunteers. None of the people who appear in the parades get paid. There are many reasons for people volunteering, but the one heard most is quite simple: "I always wanted to be in a parade."

The wall outside the parade office seems to be covered with wallpaper. A closer look reveals that it isn't wallpaper, but a series of posters painted in red and highlighted with silver sparkle dust. You can see the words from very far away, "Be a clown, be a clown, all the world loves a clown." Underneath, in small letters, the sign tells everybody where to volunteer to be a clown for the big parade.

On the wall around the corner from the parade office is another group of posters. These show one of the huge parade balloons and all the people it takes to hold it down. Under the balloon it says, "This is the place for people with muscle and pull." Once again, the small print tells everyone how and where to sign up.

There is one more poster in the series created to get people to volunteer for the parade. It too is on the wall in a spot that most people will see, right outside the employees' bathrooms in a huge department store. This one shows people doing all sorts of dancing, and in bright shiny letters it says, "Put a little fun in your life, try dancing." Then in smaller letters it says, "If you can walk or boogie, the parade is for you. Sign up now, before it's too late."

These posters are the way one parade director lets people know about the parade and the kinds of people in it. The whole idea is to make the parade seem so much fun and so

This volunteer is delighted to "be a clown"

Minneapolis Star & Tribune

exciting that everyone will want to be in it. The posters tell everyone about the parade and get everybody excited about it. Once that's done, people are not only happy to be in the parade, they beg to be able to sign up for it.

It doesn't take long for these posters to do their job. Within a week, the assistant director in charge of volunteers is able to report that they have all the people they need for the parade. More than 2,500 have signed up to do all sorts of things as part of the parade team. The director is especially delighted to find out that more than half of the people who signed up had been in the parade the year before.

Other parades, without the offices and the walls of the Macy group, get their volunteers through word of mouth. One person tells another, who tells another, and so on. The people on the floats in the Rose Parade are never celebrities. They are people who have volunteered for the job because they want to be a part of the parade. For a long time the Rose Parade directors have felt that they want viewers to have plenty of time to see all of their floats. They don't want the viewers at the parade or those at home watching on television to be more interested in the people riding on the float than in the float itself. To them and to their parade, the float and not the person or personality is important. To keep it this way, they use people who come to them or write to them asking if they can be on a float. If you write early enough and are lucky enough, you too might be riding on a beautiful float in the Tournament of Roses Parade.

As with just about everything else, parades differ when it comes to celebrities riding on floats. Some parades, like the Rose Parade, never have them, while others, like those at Thanksgiving, have well-known people on every float. And getting these personalities to give up their holiday, spend large amounts of money for plane fare and other expenses, and stand freezing on a rocking, moving float for more than two hours can sometimes be quite a challenge.

Part of the director's job is to choose and then convince the guests and celebrities to appear in each parade. Sometimes it is quite easy. You call the right person at the right time, and he or she is delighted to appear. Sometimes it takes calls all over the country and even then you strike out.

"Of course I understand that you'd love to be in the parade . . . No, I can't make any exceptions. We don't pay anyone to appear in the parade . . . Sure, I know it would cost plenty to

Members of the Village People
singing group ride on a float and sing
hits from their latest album

Donna Ruth Feinstein

fly here for the one day . . . What would I do to make it easier for you to say yes? C'mon now, you know better than that . . . Millions and millions of people will see you riding on that float. Plenty of close-ups too. How about it? Do you have a new record, a television show, or a movie coming out soon? Riding in the parade would be a great plug for any of them . . . It's good business to be in the parade and unbeatable publicity for you. What do you think?"

There is a pause as the director listens to the singer on the other end of the phone. "O.K., O.K.," says the director. "Check with your agent and call me back as soon as you know. Bye now."

Almost as soon as the director hangs up the phone, it starts to ring. It is the publicity director of a very large recording company. After the usual "Hello" and "How are you," the publicist gets to the point. He has a brand-new group with a great sound. They look good too. Something different from all the other groups. They have just cut a new album and he wonders if the parade could use the group on a float.

The parade director listens and smiles. In the last phone call she was doing the selling, now someone is selling her. The publicist continues: "This would really be a great way for us to get this group in front of an audience. Millions of people would see them. We'll make up a beautiful float, dress them in sensational costumes, and play the record as they ride on the float. Are you interested?"

The parade director waits a few seconds before answering, then says, "Sounds good to me, but does this group fit in with the theme of our parade?"

They speak on the phone for quite some time. The parade director makes some suggestions and the publicist makes some. They talk and talk, and finally have it. The float and the group will fit in perfectly with the theme of the parade. When the conversation is over, the parade director says, "That's just great. Keep me posted as things go along. I'll send a contract along for you to sign in a few days. I'll look forward to having your people in the parade."

After the phone is back on the hook, the director laughs for a moment. "I guess you win some and you lose some. That's show biz."

9

Telling the World

WHAT GOOD IS A PARADE if no one comes? Sure, some people will hear about it and come, but think about all the people who may miss all the fun. Public relations and publicity to the rescue! Though you would probably not think that a parade needs someone to tell the world about it, it does, and the person who handles this part of the effort is another very important member of the team.

There are a great many things that Jane's office handles. Some fall into the area of publicity and public relations, and some do not, but all of it makes the parade more exciting for the people in it and for the people who watch.

Jane is the press person, the instruction person, the illustration person, the badge and button person, in short, she is the person everybody comes to for anything concerning the parade that nobody else has. As the person in charge of all the graphics for the parade, she takes care of all the signs, banners, instruction sheets, badges, and buttons. She works with artists, writers, printers, painters, designers, and many other craftspersons to produce these materials. It is also her job to get and send all the invitations to the parade, to make and process all the applications, and to assign and supervise a whole army of photographers who will take pictures of the parade.

And the best part of all this is that none of it was supposed to be her job. But as she always says with a little smile, "Can't figure how it happened. This job seems, like Topsy, to have 'just growed.' But it's terrific, and you get to be really a part of this great event."

When she was hired, Jane was told to pick her staff, the people with whom she would work to produce the press kits for the media. The press kits were to be designed for people who knew the parade as well as for the people who had never seen the parade but had to tell their readers and listeners about it. These special folders are packed with pictures and information for newspaper and magazine people, for radio and television people. The whole idea is to give them all the information they need so they can tell their readers and listeners as much as possible about the parade. The kits have to be full, they have to be complete, and they have to be accurate. The idea is that if more people hear about the parade and learn something about it, more will be interested in seeing it, either in person or on television.

Some of the things that are a part of the press kit were easy to find. Jane needed a colorful, interesting photo to use on the cover of the folder. There were so many from the past year's parade, all she had to do was pick. Then she had to tell something about the balloons, the floats, the bands, and the horses in this year's parade. There are a lot of facts in the press kit, but there is also a lot of "human interest" information—details that intrigue people.

Here's the way the press kit described the horses and their riders, or as it calls them, "equestrians," for a recent Rose Parade. "It's New Year's morning, and long before dawn a steady stream of cars, vans, trucks, and trailers begin arriving in Pasadena. All have one thing in common—one or more tails protrude from the rear of each vehicle. The horses have arrived, and along with them the 200 equestrians who will ride the Arabians, Palominos, Morgans, Appaloosas, and others. Many have participated for more than twenty consecutive years . . ."

Perhaps the most important people to get the press kits are the hometown newspapers and the radio and television stations of the bands marching in the parade. Everyone at home wants to know about "their" band. This kind of writing and describing is easy for the publicity and public relations people, because, as Jane says, "Writing about a hometown band is great. We help out the small towns by giving them something that ties them to the big cities. It's their kids making good. It's great for everyone. It's great for the bands and it's great for us too."

Volunteers practice laying Poppin'
Fresh down to get under a walkway
on the parade route

Minneapolis Star & Tribune

If writing about the bands is easy, writing about some of the other parts of the parade sometimes becomes a bit more difficult. How do you tell about the floats and balloons? How do you tell about floats and balloons that people have known and seen for years and years? A good publicity person finds the words to make the balloons, for example, seem bright and fresh and new and wonderful, so people will want to come to the parade or watch it on television just to see those balloons.

Here's the way Jane told everyone about one balloon that had been flying for many years: "Red Baron, beware! Snoopy has traded in his launching pad for a Sopwith Camel and is preparing for a real dogfight.

"Everyone's favorite dog took one small step for man, one giant leap for mankind several years ago when he became an astronaut for the Macy's Thanksgiving Day Parade. After all, that was the year of the astronaut—Apollo 10's modules 'Snoopy' and 'Charlie Brown' rehearsed in a lunar environment in May, and man walked on the moon two months later.

"Although Snoopy had made his parade debut as an aviator only the year before, he was not about to be left behind. He became an astronaut too. Now, with that accomplishment under his belt, he has brushed the moon dust from his feet and put on the goggles of the famous World War I flying ace to battle the Red Baron. In this year's parade, watch for Snoopy to fly rather than orbit."

How could anyone resist seeing the "new-old" Snoopy doing his thing again?

10
Judges and Judging

THE NOISE was deafening. Hundreds of people, most of them teenagers, were crawling over and under four floats being finished in a huge, cold building for the Tournament of Roses Parade. Tomorrow would be the parade, but tonight was the judging.

Not all parades have formal float-judging and awarding of trophies and certificates. But for the parades that do, judging time is jitters time, heart-in-mouth time, "we just have to win" time.

The judges are selected from lists of prominent people who are either in the arts or in other fields that give them the eye and the experience needed for the job. In the Rose Parade, these judges will work through the night before the parade to see all of the more than sixty floats that will be taking part. They will crisscross the entire town, going from building site to building site, to be sure that each float has been visited and viewed at least three times before they give out the awards.

The first time the judges see the floats they are almost, but not quite, completed. It is about 8:00 P.M. in the evening before the parade. There are still plenty of finishing touches to add to each of the floats. That doesn't matter to the judges, who are looking to see the overall design, the way the theme is carried out, and the way the float is put together. Later on, when the floats have been completed, they will look for the

Judges had no trouble awarding this
float a prize

Tournament of Roses Association

most beautiful float, the most original float, the most humorous float, the float that makes the best use of color, the float that makes the best use of animation, and the best float from outside the United States.

Just before the judges are scheduled to arrive at a float-building site, a fast and furious cleaning job takes place. With several hundred teenagers working, there are a lot of brown paper lunch bags, thick-shake paper cups, hamburger wrappers, and other debris to go with the cut flower stems, leaves, and waste petals. In some areas it's impossible to see the floor. But it doesn't take long to sweep the place clean.

When everything is spotless, the boys and girls go back to their places to add those finishing touches to the floats. Once again the noise level rises as the float decorators and flower pasters sing and yell and clown a bit while they work.

Suddenly, the huge doors at one end of the building open and three people in white suits come in. And just as suddenly there is silence in the building. Everyone working on the floats gets off and stands quietly behind them. The judges, each carrying a clipboard with grading sheets for each float, walk up to the first float. By this time, the designer has come to the float to join them. The judges walk around the float, look under it, on top of it, and all around it. As they walk they make notes on their sheets. They ask the designer several questions, and then, as the designer walks, talks, and points, they look all over the float once again. When they are satisfied that they have enough information about the float and have seen it enough, the judges move to the next float and start all over again.

Once again the building crews swarm all over the floats. This will be their last chance to finish them, to make them exactly the way the designer intended. They don't have much time left. Soon the big doors will swing open again and the floats will be moved into their position in the middle of the street.

The final judging of each float takes place at about 3:00 A.M. on the morning of the parade. Through the night, most of the teenagers stay with "their" float, finishing the "million and one things" that still have to be done. As they finish their work they curl up in blankets on the curb and try to sleep. But, for most, the excitement is too much.

"Wake up, wake up, they're back," whispers a girl in a bright-red sweat shirt to the girl next to her. "I'm up, I'm up," the second girl says as she pokes still another girl, wrapped in a blanket, next to her. Everyone on the curb around the float is now sitting as the judges start their final walk around the float. One of the judges is a famous designer of furniture, another is an award-winning architect, and the third has been active in the florist business for more than thirty years. They have seen many other floats in past years, but this is the first time they have been asked to be judges.

Slowly the judges circle the float. They look and look and continue to make notes on their judging sheets. Although they had pretty well made up their minds after seeing the floats the other two times, they want to see the floats as millions of viewers will see them, completely finished and ready to go.

Once again there isn't a sound anywhere near the floats. The judges have stepped off to the side, a little bit away from one of the very large floats. They have their heads together and seem to be adding up the numbers written on their sheets. After what seems like hours, but is only minutes, the judges break their huddle and hand a sheet to one of the parade officials. The official takes the sheet, puts it together with some others, and announces the winners.

As each winner is announced, banners are placed next to the float. And as each winner is announced, there are cheers and screams of delight. Some of the people who worked on the winning floats yell, jump, and cry with joy. And while they do, many of the losers cry too.

The competition completed, the judges leave, the workers leave, the builders leave, all to find places where they can sit and wait and see "their" float come by in "their" parade.

11

The Magic Eyes of Television

TIMING IS THE KEY. Though it is important for all the teams putting on the great parades, it is vital for the television team. Sure, when the audience sees the parade on television, everything is right, everything is complete, and everything is on time. That's the sign of a good production. The parade seen at home looks like the parade seen on the street. Looks real easy. Looks as if the television people just set up their cameras and start shooting. That's what it's supposed to look like, but it takes a lot more than just setting up. It takes people, it takes equipment, it takes know-how—it takes a full team working very hard to make it all look very easy.

If you're a television station that sends its pictures to a single area, or a network that covers most of the country, you have to decide, before you do anything else, how you want to "cover" the parade. Do you want it to "run," to look at home exactly the way it looks to the people watching the parade on the street, or do you want it to be a "show," a production, with performers and groups doing "their thing." If the choice is to televise the parade exactly the way it looks, it must be timed so there are no gaps, no breaks in the action. If the parade is to be a show, you must know how long it takes for a float to go by, and how long the performers will be doing their numbers. Either way, preparations must get under way about six months before the parade steps off.

Setting up the cameras

Cotton Bowl Council

A real challenge to a television parade production team comes when they do more than one parade at one time. On Thanksgiving Day, for example, CBS does what it calls the All-American Thanksgiving Day Parade. In three hours the network brings parades from New York, Philadelphia, Detroit, Hawaii, and a pretaped parade of Toronto's October Thanksgiving Day parade. Describing to a parade director the way it will be televised, the CBS person in charge suggested it was like an African safari, with the elephants trunk to tail.

"What we do is to try to keep the parades head to tail, tail to head. We start in Philadelphia. By the time we are about 40 minutes into that parade, the New York parade starts.

When the New York parade is almost over, we have people with walkie-talkies telling us of the progress of the Detroit parade. Just as soon as New York ends, Detroit starts. It's the same when we put on Toronto and Hawaii. Our whole idea is to bring a parade the way it is. We help it along by seeing that there are no spaces, no gaps, no dull spots. We figure that people who are watching a parade want to see a parade, not a performance, and that's what we give them. We let the parade carry the action."

It takes hundreds of people spread all over the country and into Canada to bring to the television screen the five parades in three hours. "They really have to be a team. They must work together like the parts of a clock, or they leave us here in the control center looking a bit foolish." Added to this kind of teamwork is the kind shown by the announcers, or rather the personalities who tell the viewers and listeners about the parade.

If you've noticed that the kinds of people who "do" parades have changed, you're right, and for very good reason. For many years announcers told the viewers what they were seeing, along with some extra information. The television people soon learned that the viewers were not so interested in learning details about the floats, for example, as they were in enjoying a parade with their friends. They wanted to see the parade and listen to someone they knew, who was also having a very good time. So now, instead of "regular" announcers, you get William Conrad from *Cannon*, Loretta Swit from *M*A*S*H*, Jack Lord from *Hawaii 5-0*, and other stars like Lucy Arnez, Mike Douglas, and many, many more.

Fortunately, the networks do not have much trouble getting stars to appear on the parade telecasts. Says the executive producer, "They really want to do these jobs. Parades are for whole families. Especially on a holiday like Thanskgiving, when the whole family is home and around the set most of the time. The stars want the audience to get to know them as real people, not as the characters they play. They want to

76

be recognized by their own names. They want viewers to know them as friends who are having a good time seeing a good parade. It's just very good for everyone."

Work starts on the day after Labor Day, in September, and doesn't stop until the parade has passed by. Five writers prepare the information for the stars. The stars don't read from a final script. They can say what they want, but the network wants them to have the information so that what they are saying is accurate. Special researchers add more information, and then the producers work directly with the parade directors. The television people never tell the parade people what they can or cannot do. Instead, they give suggestions that will

Rehearsing with celebrities the day
before the parade

Cotton Bowl Council

help make the band, group, or float look even better than it already does. Once again, it's a team operation to see that everything looks and sounds the best it can.

Very often, there are special things in a parade that both the parade director and the television producers feel the audience would like to see. To be sure such things are seen without leaving something else out, there must be rehearsals and timing sessions. For example, in one parade, there was a 40-horse hitch of huge Clydesdales. It was ten rows of four horses and quite a sight. They were pulling a big circus wagon that was almost eighty years old. That too was quite a sight. Says the producer, "It really was something to see. But that's not all. The trainer had worked with them for so long and trained them so well that these 40 horses could go into reverse. Imagine 40 big beautiful horses stopping, backing up, and then going forward again. We had to run it several times in practice so we could figure out how much time to allow. We found out it takes twice as long to back up as to go forward."

There are other rehearsals too, but these take place the day before the parade. Since you can't march a parade past the cameras in rehearsal, the television people need to substitute something so they will know the best spots to put their cameras. Instead of floats they use buses, and instead of bands they use heavy traffic. The cameras are put into position and follow the buses or the cars down the street.

Several weeks before parade day, the television team completes its parade book. This is the book that gives the star everything he or she might ever want to know about everything in the parade. There are pictures of the floats with all sorts of information. There is information about the bands and the songs they will play. Whatever is in the book has been checked and can be used. At meetings with the stars, the parade directors, and the television people all of the last-minute details are discussed. Everyone gets timing sheets that detail exactly when everything is supposed to happen.

Space has been left for commercials, and space has been filled in with taped pieces if there are any gaps.

The stars are told, once again, to check with the book before they say anything on the air. The story is told of the famous singer who happily informed the whole country that the song being played by the Texas band was "I've Been Working on the Railroad." In only a few minutes the switchboard at the network had lighted up with angry Texans saying the song was "The Eyes of Texas Are Upon You."

With everything ready to go, the meeting breaks up. There are still a great many last-minute details for everyone to complete. It looks as if everything is under control, but there are always last-minute jobs. Tomorrow is the big parade, and tonight there is still plenty to do.

12

'Twas the Night Before . . .

THIS IS IT. The very last chance. Tomorrow is the day of the parade, but tonight there is still plenty to do. This is the time for the teams to come together, to become one large team. This is the time to prove the worth of their teamwork.

A final meeting is called for all the band directors with the music director. There are snacks and soft drinks, pads and pencils on the table. The band directors are in charge of more than 1,400 musicians. The music director stands up, and it gets very quiet. "If you have any questions or any problems, now is the time to ask. I will be delighted to do anything I can to help. Just try me." The meeting lasts just under two hours, and as they leave, the music director shouts, "O.K., everyone, let's give them a real show tomorrow."

In another part of town, costumes are being carefully checked and then carefully put on hangers. The clothes are in groups, according to float and according to position in the parade. There are signs above each group of costumes showing to which float they belong. For the last two days the float riders have been coming in for final fittings. The costume designers and their team have worked late into the night making costumes longer, shorter, looser, tighter. They fixed buttons and zippers. Now they are through. As they walk out of the costume storage area, one of the designers says, "Well, when do we get started on next year's parade?"

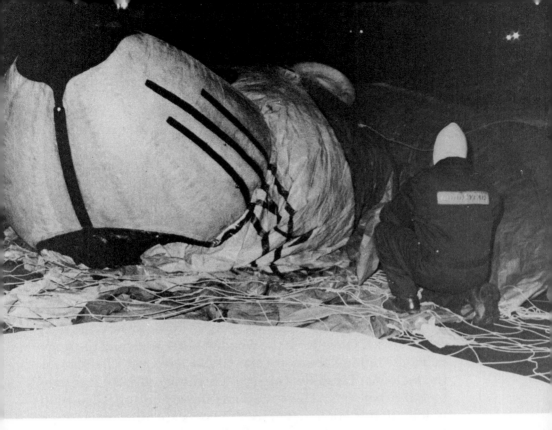

Filling the giant balloon with helium
Donna Ruth Feinstein

That's the way it goes all over town. Television crews are getting set up and running tests of their equipment. Band members are having dinner, checking out their music and uniforms for the thousandth time, and getting ready for bed. Jugglers are doing some last-minute practicing. Clowns are looking into mirrors trying to decide what would make their faces look funnier.

As soon as the director hangs up the phone, it rings again. The office looks like the command posts you see in the movies. Each of the teams is calling in to "headquarters" to tell the director its members are ready for the big day. One after another they call, check everything out, then hang up. Everything is going smoothly. Lots of time, lots of effort, lots of experience, lots of teamwork is paying off.

On a side street near the beginning of the parade, teams of people wearing coveralls are standing, waiting. There are five people in some groups, more than twenty in others. They are all cold. Suddenly one group after another turns toward the end of the street. Now there is applause. Above it all comes the cry "They're finally here. Let's set 'em up."

Huge floats are coming down the street. In moments they are in position and ready to go. Some of the floats have to be unfolded. The "arms" come out very slowly, pushed into position by several people. In a few moments, these floats look as they are supposed to look. The floats are all ready to move out into the parade.

Special floodlights all over the street turn night into day. As soon as the floats are ready, the people move toward the next set of trucks. These have the wooden boxes that hold the huge balloons. Behind them are the trucks filled with helium for the balloons. Tarpaulins are stretched over the street to protect the balloons. Then they are unpacked, unrolled, and unfolded. It is not long before the hoses are attached and the helium begins to pour into the balloons. Now they are starting to look like balloons—Snoopy, Kermit the Frog, Superman.

Huge nets are pulled over the balloons to keep them from flying up into the air. It is very cold now, but no one minds. Everything is almost ready for the big parade. This is going to be the best parade ever. It just has to be!

Up, up, and away
Goodyear Aerospace Corporation

13

Stepping Out

HUGE BUSES pull up to the curb, let off clowns, turn around and go back for another load. Captains and marshals check everyone off on their lists, tell them where to wait, then call in another busload. This one has band members, and they too go where they are told.

On the side street at the very beginning of the parade, the balloons are straining to get up and on their way. The people in coveralls stay close to their balloons, making certain everything is fine.

The celebrities arrive in a special bus. Many of them look heavier than usual. They have listened to the director and put on warm underclothing. One by one they are taken to their floats, set in position, then strapped in for safety.

It is almost time. The little electric carts with the assistant directors go from group to group, from captain to captain, from marshal to marshal, checking to see that everything and everyone is ready to go.

The bands are tuning up. The clowns are warming up. Float engines are revving up. Everything is ready. The parade director checks the stopwatch. Another thirty seconds. The police mount up and move out in a line. They stop right in front of the director.

The first band moves up, right behind the mounted police. The television cameras come to life as the little red light on

Ready to hold on? Whatever you do,
don't let go!

Donna Ruth Feinstein

top lights up. Fifteen seconds to go. The director is standing
on top of a tall television camera platform, with one hand in
the air and the other wrapped around a microphone. The
seconds tick off. Now it is time. Right on the dot. The hand
comes halfway down and one finger points forward.

"O.K., folks. This is it. Let's really give them a show. Let's
give them a parade they'll remember. Step out, please . . ."

Index

87

About the Authors

BARBARA and D. X. FENTEN have worked together as a writing team for more than twenty years, coauthoring some books and writing others independently. They have two children. The Fentens live on Long Island, New York.